Stockholm

Stockholm

Patrick Toland

Templar Poetry

Published in 2014 by Templar Poetry

Fenelon House
Kingsbridge Terrace
58 Dale Road, Matlock, Derbyshire
DE4 3NB

www.templarpoetry.com

ISBN 978-1-906285-81-4

Copyright ©

A CIP catalogue record of this book is available from the British Library

Typeset by Pliny
Printed in England

Acknowledgements

The poem 'Drive' first appeared in *Crannog* and was nominated for the Best Single Poem Forward Prize. 'Making Love to the Poet' and 'The Position' appeared in *A New Ulster Issue 17*. 'Stockholm' first appeared as part of a poetry collective at jennylewis.org.uk

CONTENTS

Drive

When coast was clear, he'd let me work
The gears from first to third and third to fifth

(My mother dozes in the back,
The engine orchestrates the sudden shifts

Of haste and pulse). Soon, we find our mutual
Pace and there is little talking. No questions

Linger in the air, no stale or febrile skirmish.
This is fathering. One mind, two hands

And all about the road from Belfast to Ardglass
Is sunlight, clean and silent like this ward

And here he's at again, my father, pressing
At my own son's hands, ordering

From fifth to third, from third to first.
Satisfied the count is right, he gives

Him over, the piston of the younger heart
Barely altering in beat and all about

The caught heat of the windows
And love with nothing left to prove

As if it was a hawk hovering above
Our slow drive home and the child slumbering.

The Silent Majority

We don't travel round en masse
Or block-book cottages or test
The patience of the teller by all
Asking to make change at once.

We don't rush the barrier
Or scale the ridge or pledge
The ruin of the vocal few.
We're silent; and this is much

The point of faint entreaty.
All hush and shush and look
Away and nod most sagely
And something like a prayer

Rises by and is never heard.
Then we're back to pressing
Collars, or mending tractors,
And all the fury of the world

Is rivalled by the sound
Of coffee making in the pot,
The mutt next door
Barking and barking and barking.

Making Love to the Poet

We want so much.

Not just to possess you
But all touch translated
Into rough language.

And never once yourself.

You are hillock, dale,
As if your fealty to the land
Was all that commended you.

You are stoat or weasel,
As if the bed was field
And you are game.

Draining to be named
Both the ocean and the fountain.
To be petal and also stem.

Puzzling to be light falling
And dawn beckoning.
Then there is your skin -

Skin, we'll say, like a journey's end.
That one is most befuddling.
For if love is destination,

It is not through dene or glen or vale,
But you beside us, balancing the map,
Certain of arrival.

Stockholm

My father says the worst part
Of getting old is the lack of dreams

And he seems, suddenly, like a pale
Northerner too absent from the sun.

Not dreams of cadillacs or fortunes found.
Not flying, or skipping buses

Or discovered naked in your boss's office.
He misses the whole shebeen of dreams;

The whole kaleidoscopic, panopolic
Parade of what he'd ever seen

Or done or thought to dream of doing.
Days pass after that regard

And I wash his suit and thaw
His meals and never think to think

I was part of the dream.
How some of me extinguished also

Like a burning bin and all remains.
Worse than this, I've become the worm

That visits every day and gnaws
Away at what he can't recall,

Who draws it from him like a thorn.
And still, he sleeps the night

Like a grey mizzle, like a hood
That sneaks the passing light

Of alleyways and market stalls
And unfamiliar smells and the strange

Calls of a kind abductor
Who speaks softly and knows his fear.

The Position

And after the interview,
They turn to ask — and you,
Do you have any questions?

I scan my thoughts for charts,
Sheets, quarterly projections,

But all I come up with is -
How do I get him to let
My heart climb inside his heart

Like a pearl to a clam,
Like a doll back to its mother doll?

How do I ask the man in the red braces;
This morning, did you make your
Father laugh, laugh so deliriously,

That he wept, had to be held
Again until he remembered laughter?
I feel, already, I have known

Him for forty years.
Finally, I ask a question
(something about floor space/ office dimensions)

And the man says, yes, and sensing sameness
Tells me, 'but there are many windows'.

We Travel by Night

They've rung to say
My luggage has been found.

Sets you wondering
What other things have chosen
To rebel against their purpose.

Today, a leather hold-all slunk
Across a field, sherpa-like,
And earmuffed itself back

Remorsefully to a cow.
Tomorrow, a pacemaker
Will burst a chest wall,

Find a rock pool and live
Incognito as a clam.
Even a paper-clip

Dreams with much tenacity.
They knock my door
And hand the luggage over

And, for an instance,
You'd think to hear the trouser press
Sigh to search out borders

Just beyond the room.
The headed paper gasp
As you seek it out

To write of love while
The bible slumbers.

Even the Flowers Do Not Know their True Names

At last, my father

Has stopped talking to the marigolds-
Who even though they strike a pose

Of wisdom, do not seem to have the answers
To the big questions. He has turned instead

To a mulberry bush and begins
His thesis on the manners of children.

But, yet again, its solutions
Seemed trite and slightly unforgiving.

Even the daisies, with their bright
Faces, waiting to be taught, are given

To shrug and well ignore
His jabbering and coveting the garden.

I think he may find a true friend
In that flower that brims the chimney,

The lone dandelion who must
Wonder how its seed could drift

So far to settle in a roof and finds
Itself straining to hear his voice

Or catch those eyes that skim
And fold only the flat present,

The border of lilies that froths
And spills like the edge of the world.

The Beautiful Girl

Here she is — the beautiful girl
Laughing at herself.

Says her teeth are crooked
And her nose is like a bin

That's been attacked by crows.
She says her elbows

Are fallen socks and her
Eyes cross and when the doors

Close she paws for glasses
And reads in brightest light.

Of course, we all laugh at her humility
For we have not forgotten

That she is beautiful.
Then we are out into winter snow

And steadying ourselves
And holding on to low walls

And looking in on parlours
Glowing and them looking out

And smiling at our scissor
Gait and dented pride.

Suddenly we are all
Beautiful girls;

Hiding the smile we say
Is not dazzling, holding

To an arm in case we fall
And prove ourselves truthful.

RSVP

More and more I send to friends
Apologies for not attending
Fairs, or get-togethers, or those kinds
Of sitting downs and chatting round
Your histories like ribboned children.

I simply say my father's 'on the turn'
And feel most sad to think him milk
Or double-spy or souring in his views.
They understand. They always do.
And back I go to wondering

If someone missed Antoinette's
Beheading and sent, like me, a note
To speak of father's malady
And went downstairs and stirred
The stew and listened to his breathing.

Leavings

I've watched two loved ones go.

One, like a child dragged off
Before they'd blown their candles.
One like a rummy sheriff
Who'd given up fighting for the law.

If I've learnt one thing, it's this;
What you do in life, you do in death.

So, if you are called to the feast,
Lean both elbows on the table.
Lick the whole plate clean.